Read, Sort & Write
PHONICS

by Pamela Chanko

New York • Toronto • London
Auckland • Sydney • New Delhi • Hong Kong

Cover and interior design by Michelle H. Kim
Images © Scholastic Inc., Shutterstock, The Noun Project

ISBN: 978-1-338-60648-5

Scholastic Inc., 557 Broadway, New York, NY 10012
Copyright © 2020 by Scholastic Inc.
Published by Scholastic Inc.
All rights reserved. Printed in the U.S.A.
First printing, January 2020.

2 3 4 5 6 7 8 9 10   40   26 25 24 23 22 21

CONTENTS

Introduction 4

How to Use this Book 5

Customization Tools 6

Helpful Word Lists 7

Meeting the Standards 9

VOWELS

Short *a*/Long *a*
a, a_e 10
a, ai 13

Short *e*/Long *e*
e, ee 16
e, ea 19

Short *i*/Long *i*
i, i_e 22
i, igh 25

Short *o*/Long *o*
o, o_e 28
o, oa 31

Short *u*/Long *u*
u, u_e 34

CONSONANT DIGRAPHS
sh, ch 37
th, wh 40

CONSONANT BLENDS

r blends
br, cr 43
gr, tr 46

l blends
bl, cl 49
pl, sl 52

s blends
sp, st 55
sw, str 58

Create Your Own 61

Blank Sorting Templates 63

INTRODUCTION

Welcome to *Read, Sort, and Write*. These darling activity books are tons of fun—but they also build essential skills! Every book in the *Read, Sort, and Write* series builds the following skills:

- fine motor (cutting, pasting)
- sorting
- reading
- writing

Read, Sort, and Write: Phonics is a delightful way to teach kids the common sounds and spelling patterns they are likely to encounter in their reading material, both now and in the future, in order to help them become fluent readers. But what exactly *is* phonics? It is the relationship between letters and sounds, between the spoken sounds of language and the written letters that represent them. And research shows that it is an essential element in any literacy program.

SO WHY IS DIRECT PHONICS INSTRUCTION SO NECESSARY?

★ **IT IMPROVES CHILDREN'S DECODING SKILLS.** Once children learn about the power of a silent *e* (which can change *mad* to *made*), it can help them recognize other short and long vowel sounds with this pattern, like *bit/bite* and *hop/hope*. Once they learn that the letters *ch* can make the first sound in *cheese*, the better they are able to read words like *chair* and *chalk*. By teaching children to recognize spelling patterns, decoding is made far simpler.

★ **IT BOOSTS COMPREHENSION.** When decoding words becomes easier, children have more mental energy to spend on the ultimate goal of literacy: understanding the words! Children who need a long time to decode, or "sound out," every part of every word in a sentence are likely to have forgotten the first word by the time they get to the last. By then, the meaning has been lost.

★ **IT IMPROVES FLUENCY, SPELLING, AND WRITING.** Repeated practice with common sound-spelling patterns (also called phonic elements) helps children build sight word vocabulary so that they become more fluent readers. As they learn more phonic elements, the more words children are able to spell. And of course, phonics helps children become increasingly familiar with the way words work—making them better writers, as well!

It's clear that phonics instruction is essential to reading success. On the other hand, studying and memorizing lists of words is no fun. That's where *Read, Sort, and Write: Phonics* comes in. With this book, kids get to play with pumpkins, sort fish, and even stack ice cream scoops—all while building the essential skills they need for becoming great readers!

HOW TO USE THIS BOOK

THE BASICS

Using the thematic patterns is fun and easy! For every two phonic elements, there are three pages:

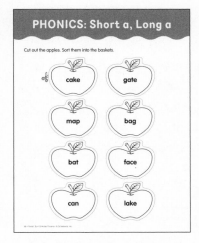

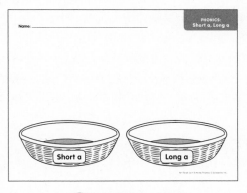

1 sorting pieces   **2** sorting mat   **3** writing practice page

Simply copy all three sheets and have kids cut out the pieces. Then have children sort the pieces onto the mat by sorting the words into the correct categories. Afterward, they can practice writing each word on the practice sheet.

FLEXIBLE USES AND FUN VARIATIONS

The activities in this book are designed for maximum flexibility.
Here are just a few tips and ideas:

- Let children color the sorting mat and pieces with crayon. Provide them with lighter shades so the words show through. If children want a permanent piece of artwork, they can glue the pieces down.

- Laminate the mat and pieces for durability. You can keep them in a storage envelope for a puzzle-like sorting activity that kids can do again and again. Keep track of your phonics puzzles by labeling the envelopes with the phonic elements they contain.

- The sorting activities and writing practice pages can be set up as an option for center time, or they can be done as seat work. You can also send them home for children to complete with family members, or as homework.

- Have children do the activities independently, or with a partner.

See the following pages for even more ways to customize the activities.

CUSTOMIZATION TOOLS

The patterns in this book contain some of the most common sound/spelling patterns, including long and short vowels, consonant digraphs, and consonant blends. On the ready-to-go patterns, we've provided 4–8 words for each phonic element—but there are many more to choose from!

On pages 7 and 8, you'll find extended word lists for each phonics element. On pages 61 and 62, you'll find blank cookies and a cookie jar template. This way you can focus on additional phonics elements. On pages 63 and 64, you'll find blank sorting pieces for every pattern in this book. This way you can expand each sorting activity to contain more pieces (and more words). You can also differentiate the activities to meet different students' skill levels. Some students may be ready for more sophisticated words, while some may need pieces with simpler ones.

HERE'S HOW TO CUSTOMIZE THE PATTERNS:

1. Choose your phonic elements from the table of contents. Make a note of the page number.

2. Find the sorting piece with the matching page number and make copies. (You can cut out the pieces that go with your mat, and save the rest for later.)

3. Write any words you choose from the appropriate word lists.

4. Add them to your sorting activity and you're ready to go!

DIFFERENTIATION TIPS

Every teacher knows that one size does not fit all! Here are some tips for leveling the activities according to students' needs.

BEGINNING LEARNERS: Divide the activity into two parts: preparing and doing. Pair children up to cut out the pieces and color them with light shades of crayon. They can also color the mat. The next day, the pair can do the activity, and take turns writing the words on the practice sheet.

INTERMEDIATE LEARNERS: As children place each word, they can read the word quietly aloud. Have them use the writing practice sheet for self-assessment—they can focus primarily on words that gave them trouble.

ADVANCED LEARNERS: Create a challenge with a timer! See if children can sort all the words in a certain amount of time. They can also time how long it takes them to write all the words. Then they can write the words again, trying to beat their own time.

HELPFUL WORD LISTS

The patterns in this book contain words with common sound/spelling patterns. Here are additional words for each phonic element in this book.

VOWELS

Short a			Long a (a_e)		Long a (ai)	Short e			Long e (ee)		Long e (ea)	
back	gasp	pack	bake	race	bait	beg	kept	sell	bee	need	beach	mean
bad	hand	pants	came	rake	fail	belt	led	sent	beep	peek	bead	neat
basket	has	pat	case	sale	faint	bench	left	set	deep	peel	beak	pea
cab	hat	rag	cave	same	pail	bend	let	tell	deer	peep	beat	peach
camp	jam	ran	date	save	raise	best	men	ten	feed	see	deal	reach
cap	land	rap	fade	take	laid	bet	mess	tent	feel	seem	feast	read
cast	lap	rash	game	tape	sail	deck	met	rest	jeep	teeth	heal	real
damp	mad	sack	gave	trace	maid	den	neck	web	meet	weed	heat	sea
dash	man	sad	late	vase	tail	desk	nest	well			jeans	seal
fact	mash	tack	make	wake	paid	fed	peg	went			lead	seat
fan	mask	tap	name	wave	waist	fell	pet	wet			leak	tea
fast	match	van	page		pail	get	red	yell			leash	teach
gas	nap	wag				help	rest	yes			meal	team

Short i			Long i (i_e)		Long i (igh)	Short o		Long o (o_e)	Long o (oa)	Short u			Long u (u_e)
big	hit	pin	bite	mine	fight	bop	mom	bone	coal	bug	dust	mud	fume
bit	kick	pit	dive	nice	might	cot	nod	cone	coat	bump	fun	mug	fuse
dip	kiss	rich	fine	nine	right	dock	not	doze	foam	bun	gum	must	mule
dish	lick	rip	five	pipe	sight	dot	pond	hole	goal	bunch	hum	mutt	muse
fib	lid	sill	hide	rice	tight	fog	pop	hope	goat	but	hush	nut	mute
fill	list	sink	hike	rise		got	rob	hose	load	buzz	hut	pup	
fish	lit	sip	life	side		hog	rod	joke	loaf	cub	jug	rug	
fit	miss	tip	like	size		hop	rot	nose	loan	cut	jump	run	
fix	mix	wig	line	time		job	sob	poke	moan	dug	just	rush	
gift	pick	win	mile	wide		jog	sock	pole	roast	dull	luck	such	
gill	pig	wish				lock	tock	rode	soak	dumb	lump	sun	
hill	pill	zip				lot	top	vote	toast	dunk	much	tug	

CONSONANT DIGRAPHS

sh				ch			th		wh	
shack	share	shin	short	chain	chase	chicken	thaw	three	whack	whine
shade	sharp	shine	shout	chair	chat	child	theater	thread	wham	whirl
shadow	shed	shirt	shovel	chalk	cheap	chilly	thief	throw	wheat	whisker
shake	sheep	shock	show	change	cheerful	chirp	thimble	thumb	where	whisper
shall	sheet	shoe	shower	chapter	cherry	choose	think	thump	which	whistle
shame	shelf	shop	shut	charge	chest	chop	thirsty	thunder	while	why
shape	shift	shore	shy	chart	chew	chuckle				

CONSONANT BLENDS

	br		cr		gr			tr	
r blends	braid	bridge	crack	croak	grab	green	grouch	trace	trip
	brain	bright	craft	crop	graph	grew	group	track	truck
	brake	bring	crawl	cross	grasp	grill	growl	trade	true
	branch	brisk	crayon	crowd	gravy	grin	grown	trail	trunk
	brand	broad	creek	crown	gray	grind	grump	train	trust
	brave	broke	creep	crunch	grease	grip		trash	truth
	break	brook	cricket	crust	great			tree	try
	breeze	brown	cried					trick	

	bl		cl		pl		sl	
l blends	blame	blind	clam	clink	plaid	pleat	slam	slime
	blank	blip	clang	clip	plain	pledge	slant	sling
	blanket	blizzard	clash	clomp	plan	plenty	slap	slip
	blast	bloom	clasp	close	planet	plink	sleepy	slipper
	blaze	blossom	claw	closet	plank	plot	sleet	slope
	bleep	blot	clay	cloth	plate	plow	sleeve	slot
	blend	blue	clean	cloud	player	plug	slice	slow
	blew	blush	clear	club	plead	plum	slick	slug
			click	cluck	please	plump	slid	slump
			cliff	clue			slide	slush
			cling	clump			slight	sly

	sp		st			sw		str	
s blends	space	spell	stack	stare	stink	swam	sweep	straight	strict
	spark	spend	stage	start	stir	swamp	swift	strain	strike
	speak	spoil	stain	state	stone	swap	swish	strand	strip
	speck	sponge	stair	steam	stool	swat	switch	strange	stripe
	speech	sport	stall	stem	stoop	sway	swoop	stray	stroll
	speed	spy	stamp	stew	storm	sweat		streak	strong
			stand	stick	story			stream	struck
			star	still	stove			stretch	

MEETING THE STANDARDS

Read, Sort, and Write: Phonics is aligned with the Common Core State Standards in English Language Arts. See how this resource supports grade K–2 standards through the strands of foundational reading and writing skills.

READING: FOUNDATIONAL SKILLS

KINDERGARTEN
PRINT CONCEPTS:
RF.K.1 Demonstrate understanding of the organization and basic features of print.
RF.K.1.B Recognize that spoken words are represented in written language by specific sequences of letters.

PHONOLOGICAL AWARENESS:
RF.K.2 Demonstrate understanding of spoken words, syllables, and sounds (phonemes).

PHONICS AND WORD RECOGNITION:
RF.K.3 Know and apply grade-level phonics and word analysis skills in decoding words.
RF.K.3.B Associate the long and short sounds with the common spellings (graphemes) for the five major vowels.

GRADE 1
PRINT CONCEPTS:
RF.1.1 Demonstrate understanding of the organization and basic features of print.
RF.1.3 Know and apply grade-level phonics and word analysis skills in decoding words.

PHONOLOGICAL AWARENESS:
RF.1.2 Demonstrate understanding of spoken words, syllables, and sounds (phonemes).
RF.1.2.A Distinguish long from short vowel sounds in spoken single-syllable words.
RF.1.2.B Orally produce single-syllable words by blending sounds (phonemes), including consonant blends.

PHONICS AND WORD RECOGNITION:
RF.1.3 Know and apply grade-level phonics and word analysis skills in decoding words.
RF.1.3.A Know the spelling-sound correspondences for common consonant digraphs.
RF.1.3.B Decode regularly spelled one-syllable words.
RF.1.3.C Know final -e and common vowel team conventions for representing long vowel sounds.

GRADE 2
PHONICS AND WORD RECOGNITION:
RF.2.3 Know and apply grade-level phonics and word analysis skills in decoding words.
RF.2.3.A Distinguish long and short vowels when reading regularly spelled one-syllable words.
RF.2.3.B Know spelling-sound correspondences for additional common vowel teams.

LANGUAGE

KINDERGARTEN
CONVENTIONS OF STANDARD ENGLISH:
L.K.1.A Print many upper-and lowercase letters.
L.K.2 Demonstrate command of the conventions of standard English capitalization, punctuation, and spelling when writing.
L.K.2.C Write a letter or letters for most consonant and short-vowel sounds (phonemes).
L.K.2.D Spell simple words phonetically, drawing on knowledge of sound-letter relationships.

GRADE 1
CONVENTIONS OF STANDARD ENGLISH:
L.1.1.A Print all upper-and lowercase letters.

L.1.2 Demonstrate command of the conventions of standard English capitalization, punctuation, and spelling when writing.
L.1.2.D Use conventional spelling for words with common spelling patterns and for frequently occurring irregular words.
L.1.2.E Spell untaught words phonetically, drawing on phonemic awareness and spelling conventions.

GRADE 2
L.2.2 Demonstrate command of the conventions of standard English capitalization, punctuation, and spelling when writing.
L.2.2.D Generalize learned spelling patterns when writing words.

Cut out the apples. Sort them into the baskets.

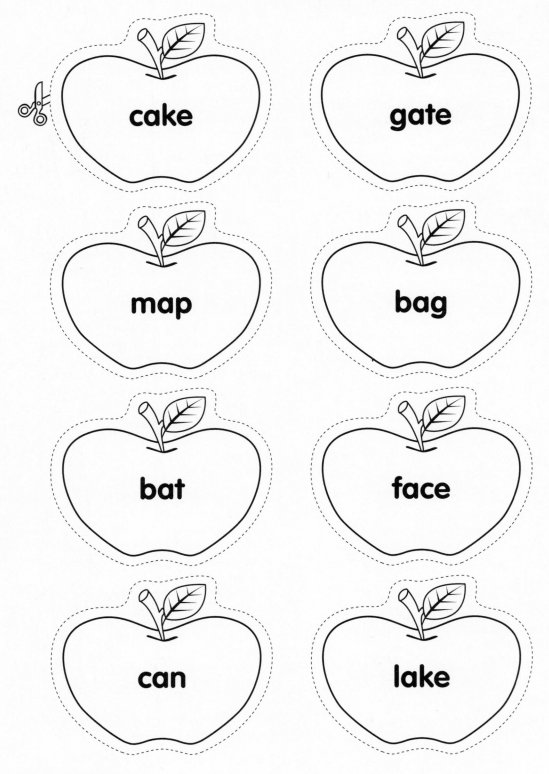

cake

gate

map

bag

bat

face

can

lake

Name: _____

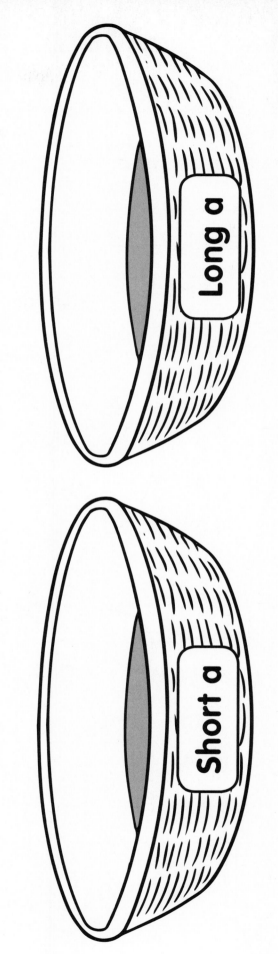

Short a

Long a

Name: _____

Trace then write each word.

bat

can

map

bag

cake

face

gate

lake

PHONICS: Short a, Long a

Cut out the pumpkins. Sort them onto the vines.

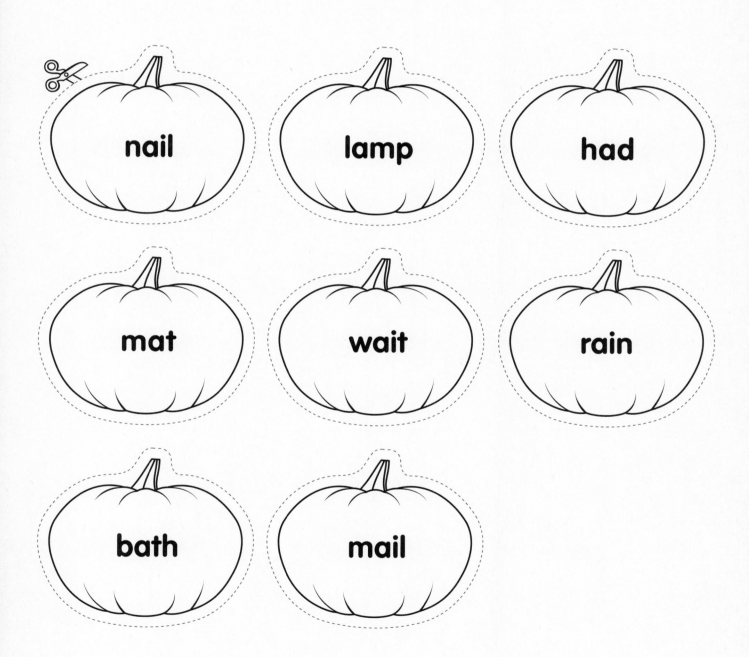

nail

lamp

had

mat

wait

rain

bath

mail

Name: _____

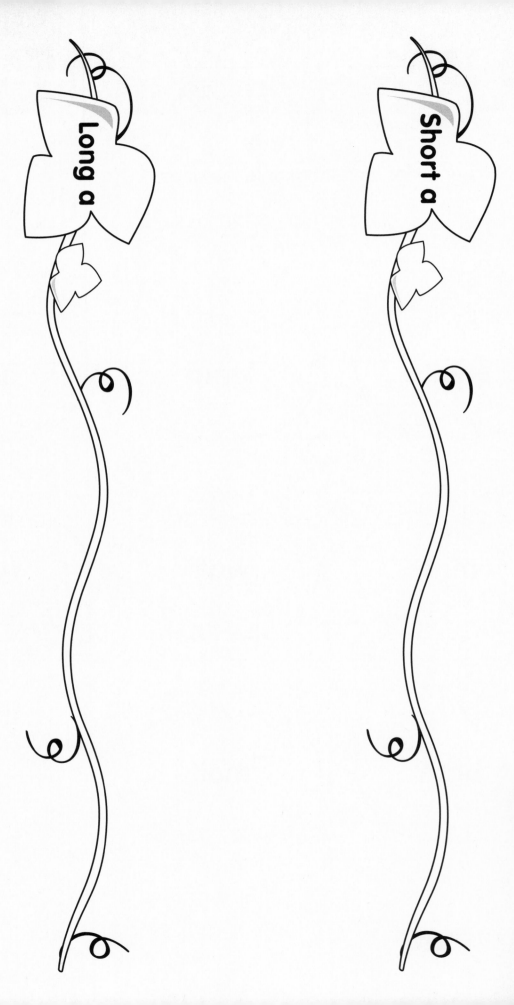

Short a

Long a

PHONICS:
Short a, Long a

Name: _____

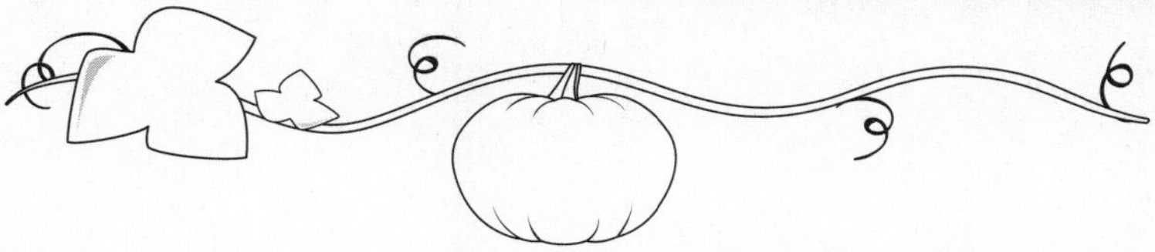

Trace then write each word.

had

lamp

bath

mat

mail

rain

wait

nail

PHONICS: Short e, Long e

Cut out the spiders. Sort them onto the webs.

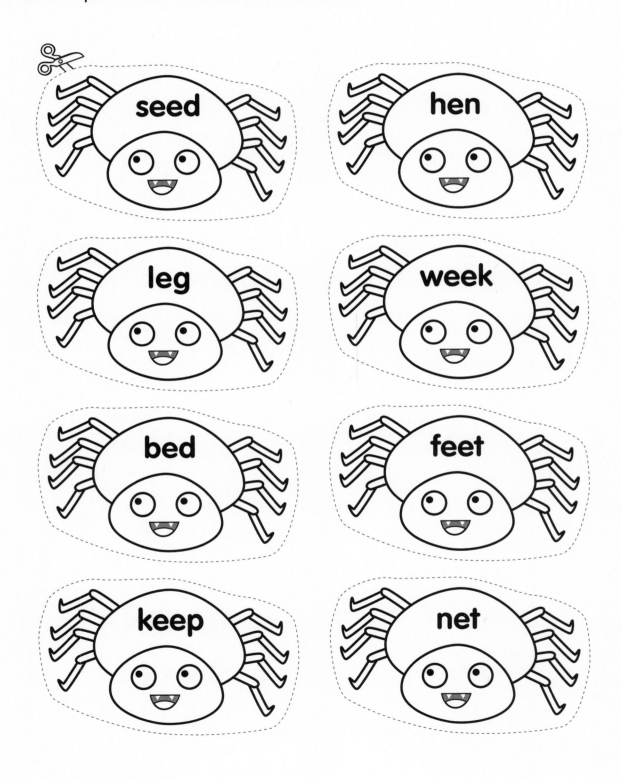

Name: _____

Long e

Short e

Name: _____

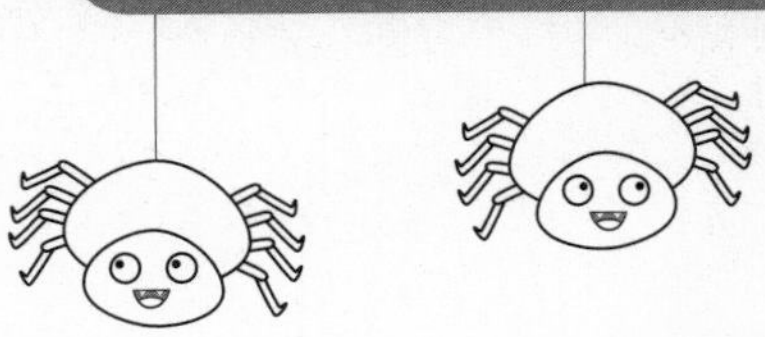

Trace then write each word.

bed

hen

net

leg

feet

seed

keep

week

PHONICS: Short e, Long e

Cut out the bats. Sort them into the caves.

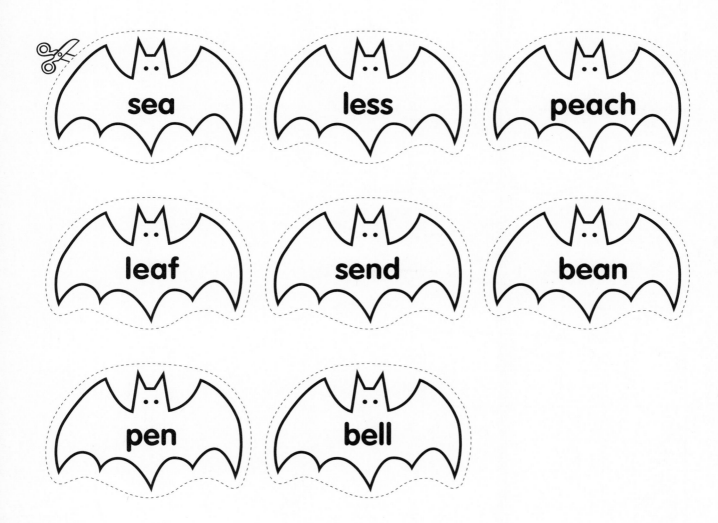

Name: _____

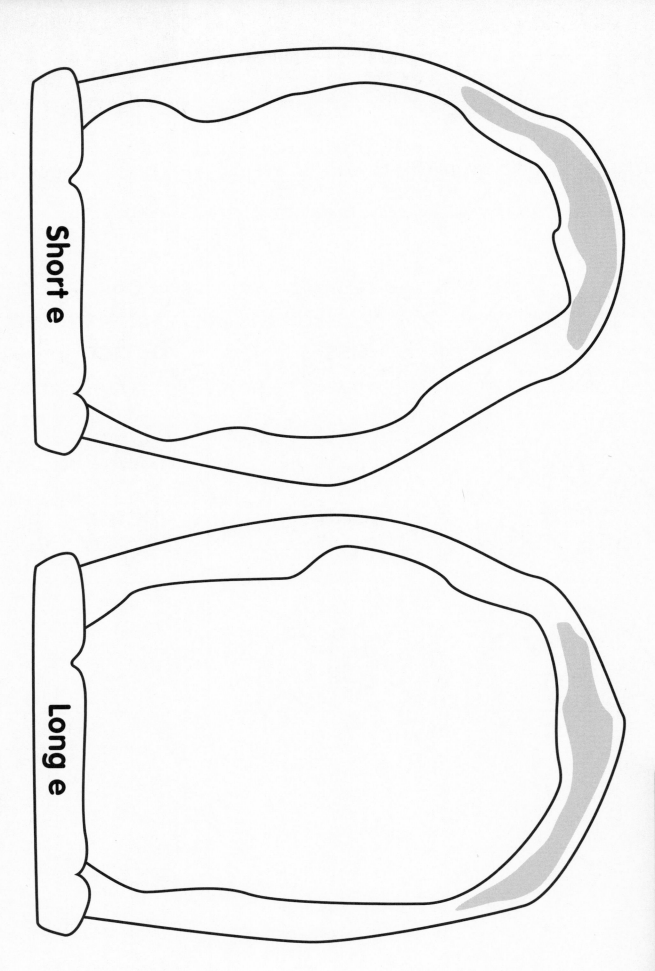

Short e

Long e

Name: _____

Trace then write each word.

bell

less

pen

send

leaf

bean

peach

sea

PHONICS: Short i, Long i

Cut out the penguins. Sort them onto the ice floes.

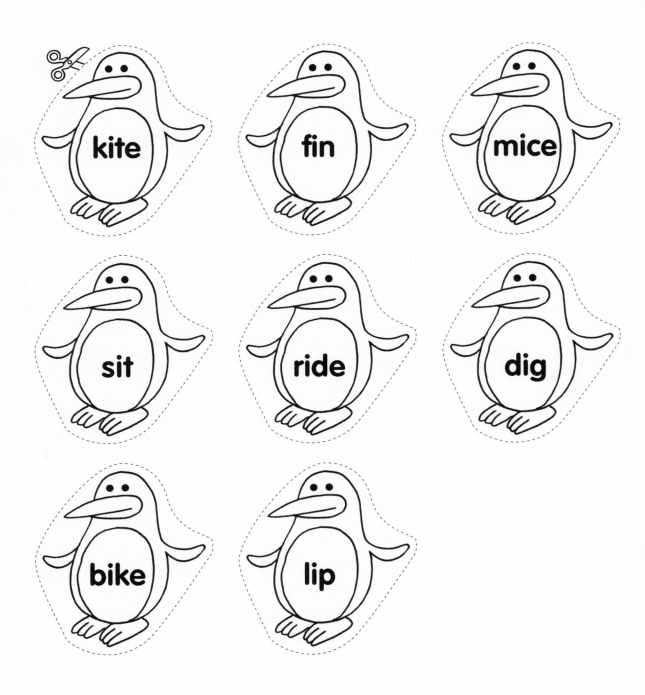

kite

fin

mice

sit

ride

dig

bike

lip

Name: _____

Short i

Long i

Name: _____

Trace then write each word.

dig

fin

sit

lip

bike

kite

mice

ride

PHONICS: Short i, Long i

Cut out the bows. Sort them onto the presents.

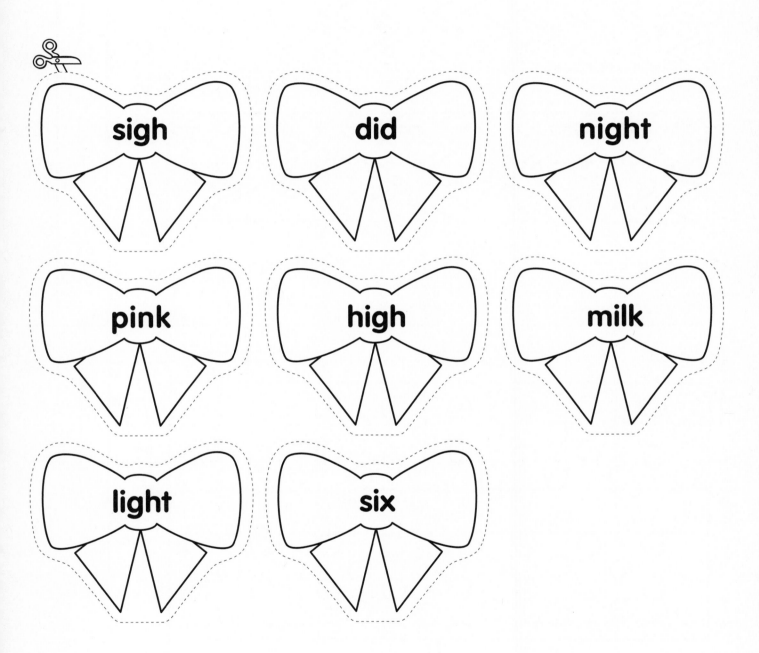

sigh

did

night

pink

high

milk

light

six

Short i

Long i

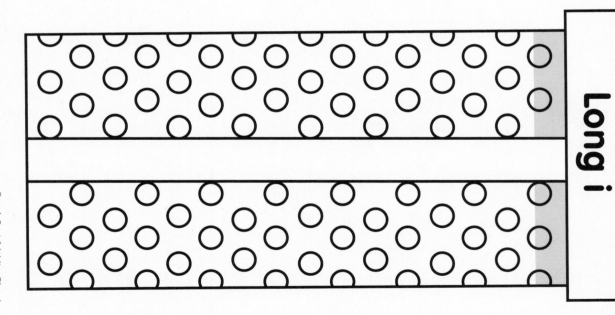

Name: _____

Trace then write each word.

did

six

milk

pink

high

light

night

sigh

PHONICS: Short o, Long o

Cut out the raindrops. Sort them under the rain cloud.

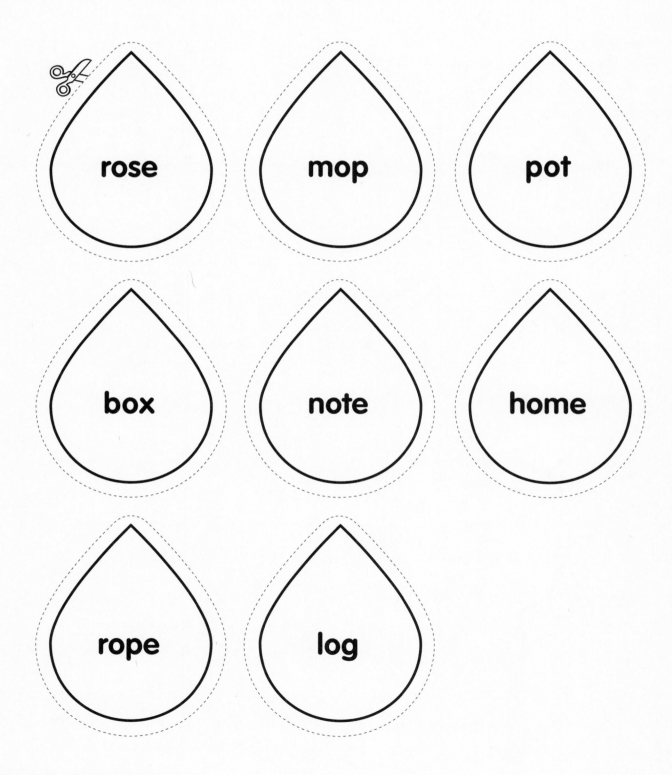

rose

mop

pot

box

note

home

rope

log

Name: _____

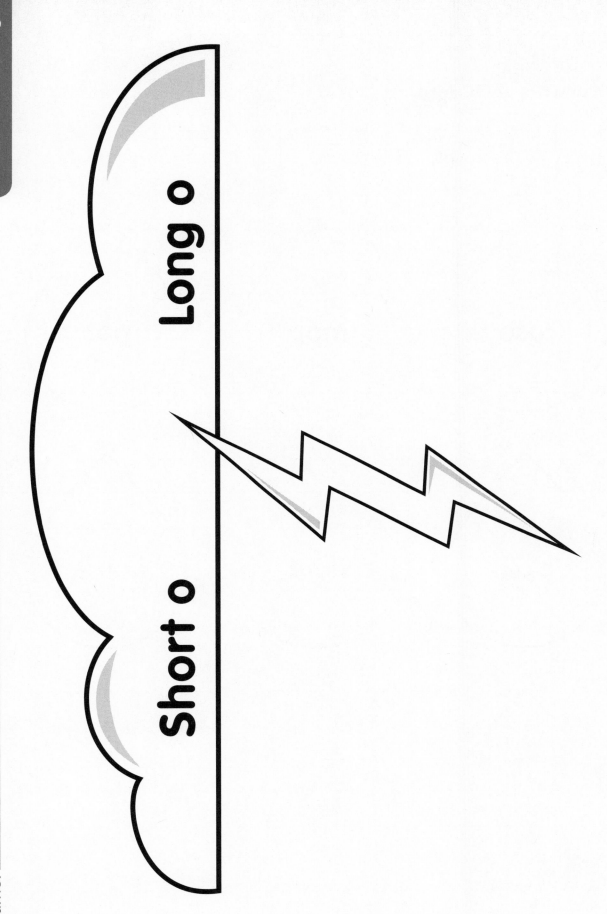

Short o

Long o

Name: _____

Trace then write each word.

log _____

pot _____

mop _____

box _____

home _____

rose _____

note _____

rope _____

PHONICS: Short o, Long o

Cut out the flowers. Sort them onto the stems.

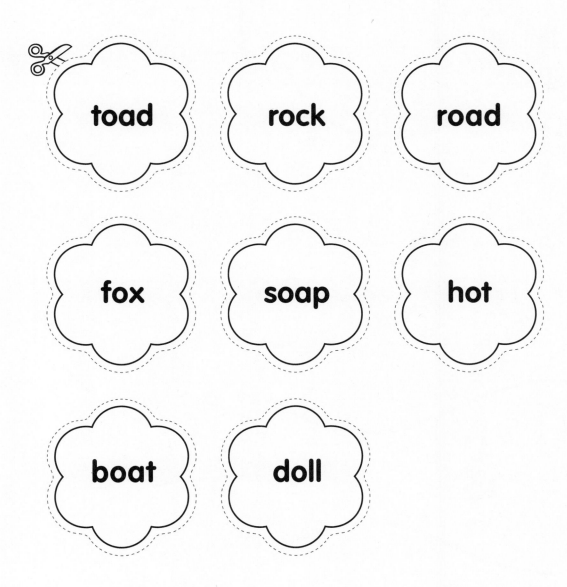

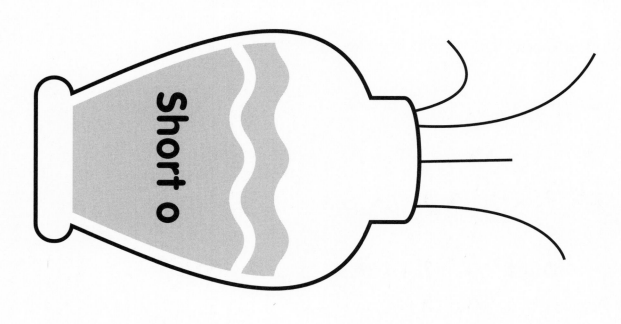

Short o

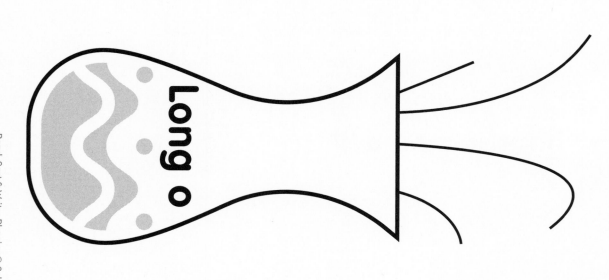

Long o

Name: _____

Trace then write each word.

hot ------------------------------

rock

doll

fox

boat ------------------------------

toad ------------------------------

soap

road ------------------------------

Cut out the bows. Sort them onto the kite strings.

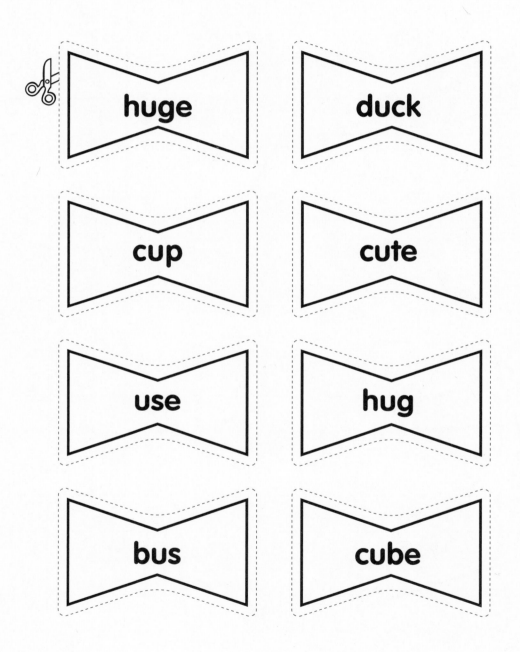

huge

duck

cup

cute

use

hug

bus

cube

Name: _____

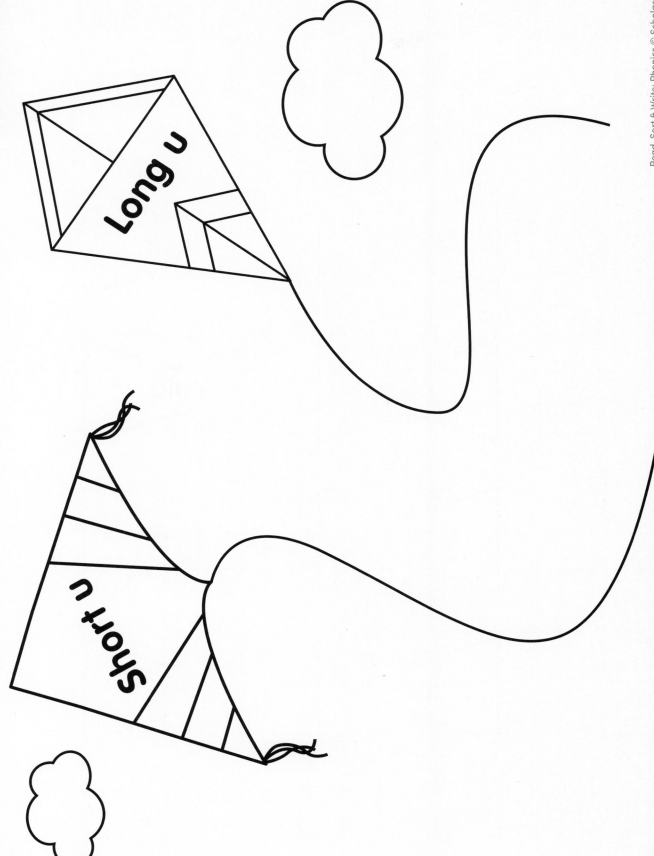

Long u

Short u

Name: _____

Trace then write each word.

bus

duck

cup

hug

use

cute

huge

cube

PHONICS: sh, ch

Cut out the bubbles. Sort them above the bubble wands.

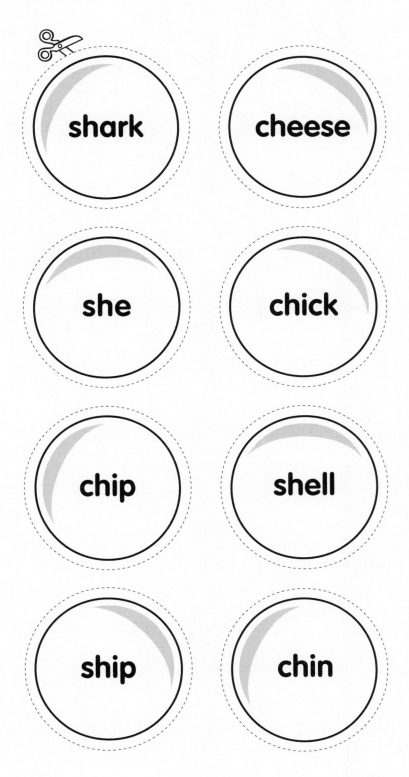

**PHONICS:
sh, ch**

Name: _____

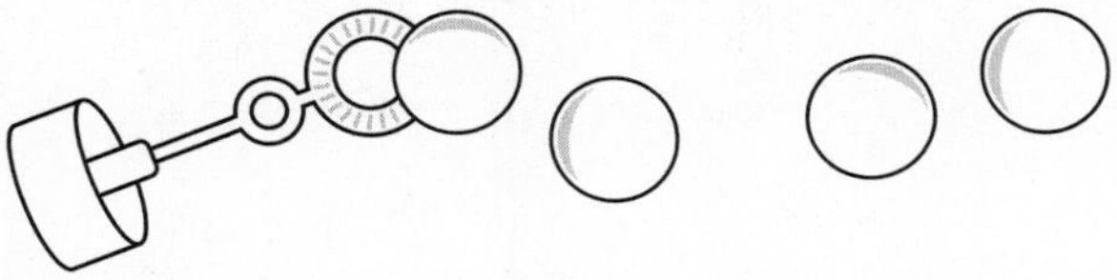

Trace then write each word.

shark

ship

she

shell

chip

chick

chin

cheese

Cut out the chicks. Sort them under the hens.

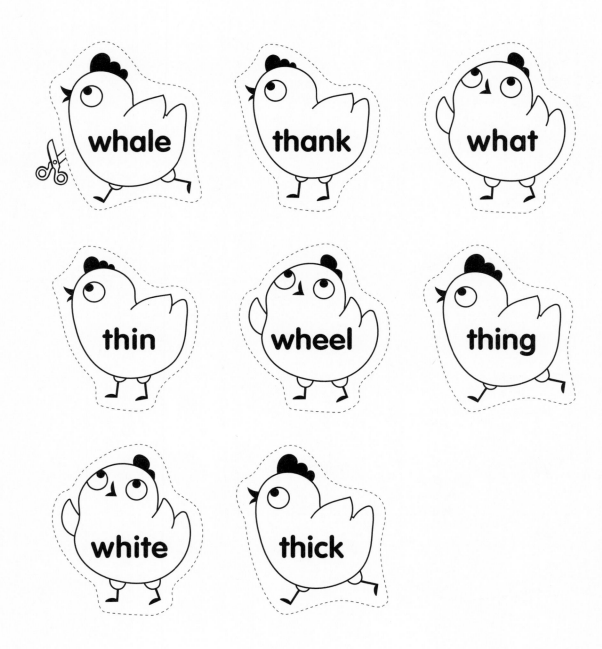

Name: _____

wh

th

Name: _____

Trace then write each word.

thing _

thank _ _ _ _ _ _ _ _ _ _ _ _ _ _ _ _ _ _ _

thick _

thin _

what _

wheel _ _ _ _ _ _ _ _ _ _ _ _ _ _ _ _ _ _ _

whale _ _ _ _ _ _ _ _ _ _ _ _ _ _ _ _ _ _ _

white _ _ _ _ _ _ _ _ _ _ _ _ _ _ _ _ _ _ _

PHONICS: br, cr

Cut out the bugs. Sort them onto the leaves.

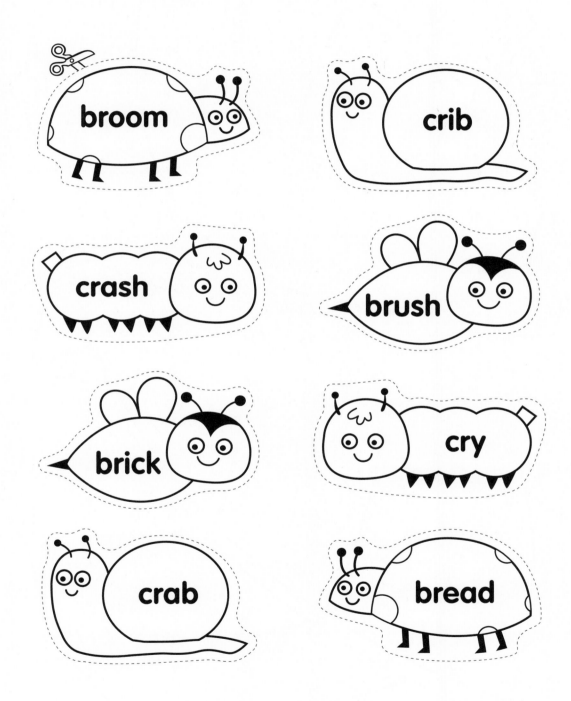

broom

crib

crash

brush

brick

cry

crab

bread

Name: _____

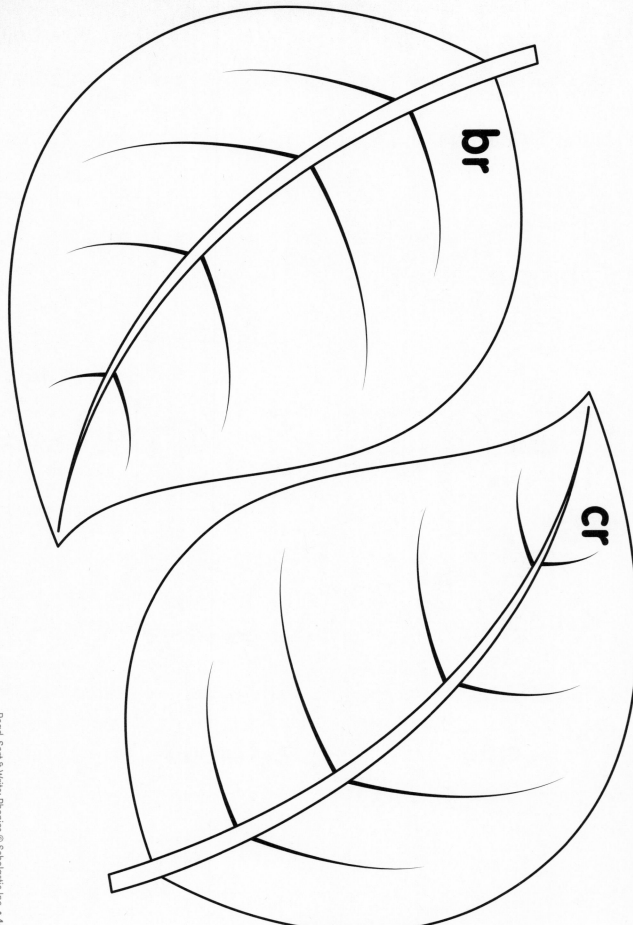

Name: _____

Trace then write each word.

bread

brick

broom

brush

crab

crib

cry

crash

Cut out the fish. Sort them into the pond.

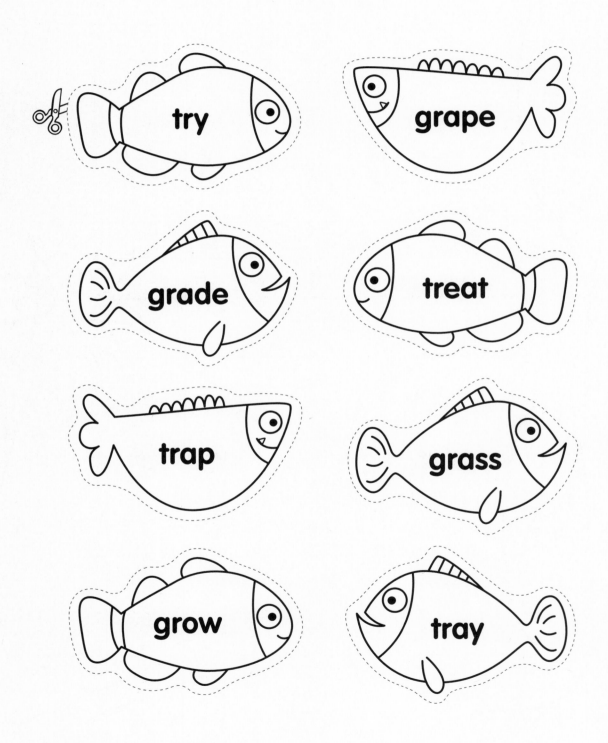

Name: _____

tr

gr

Name: _____

Trace then write each word.

grass

grape

grow

grade

trap

tray

treat

try

PHONICS: bl, cl

Cut out the seashells. Sort them onto the sand.

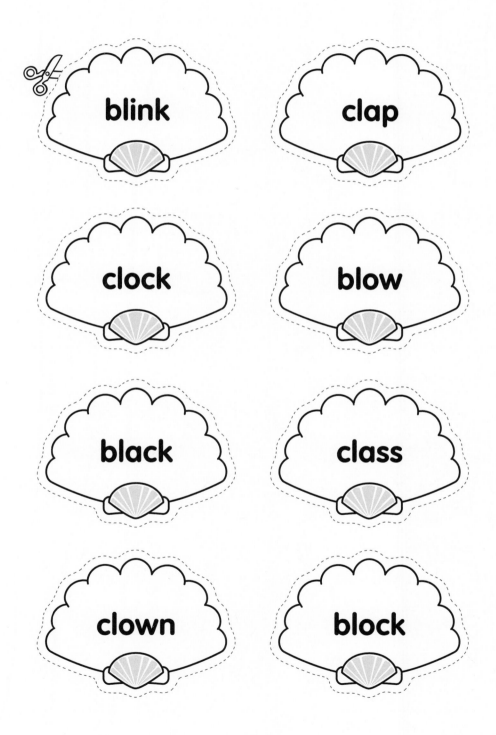

blink

clap

clock

blow

black

class

clown

block

bl

cl

PHONICS:
bl, cl

Name: _____

Trace then write each word.

block ----------------------------

blink ----------------------------

black ----------------------------

blow -----------------------------

clock ----------------------------

clap -----------------------------

class ----------------------------

clown ----------------------------

PHONICS: pl, sl

Cut out the ice cream scoops. Sort them into the cones.

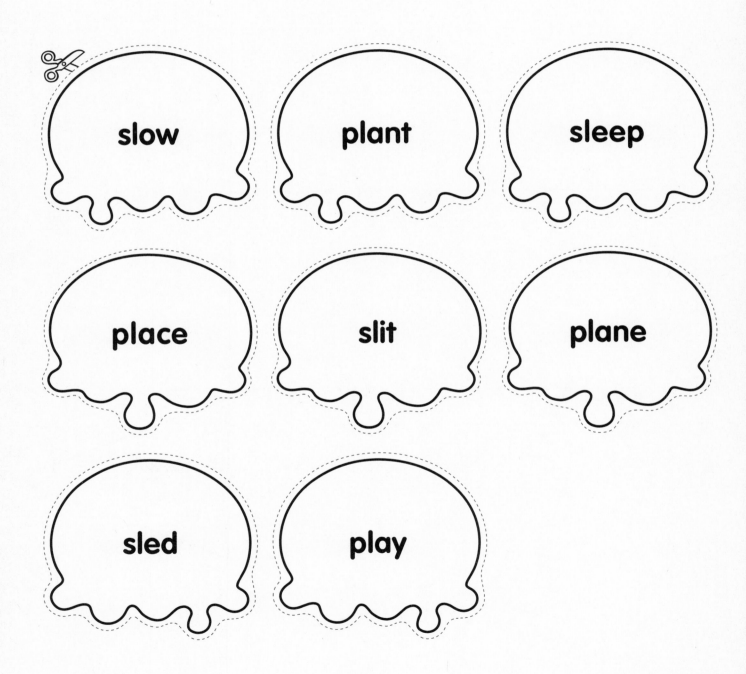

slow

plant

sleep

place

slit

plane

sled

play

Name: _____

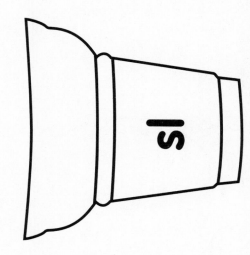

sl

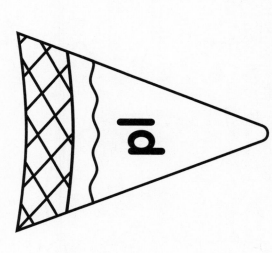

pl

Name: _____

Trace then write each word.

play

plant

plane

place

sled

sleep

slit

slow

Cut out the balls. Stack them on top of the seals' noses.

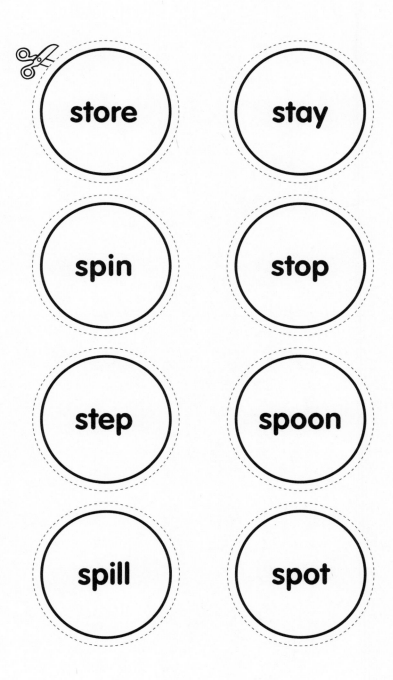

store

stay

spin

stop

step

spoon

spill

spot

Name: _____

Trace then write each word.

spot

spoon

spin

spill

stay

step

stop

store

PHONICS: sw, str

Cut out the biscuits. Sort them into the dog bowls.

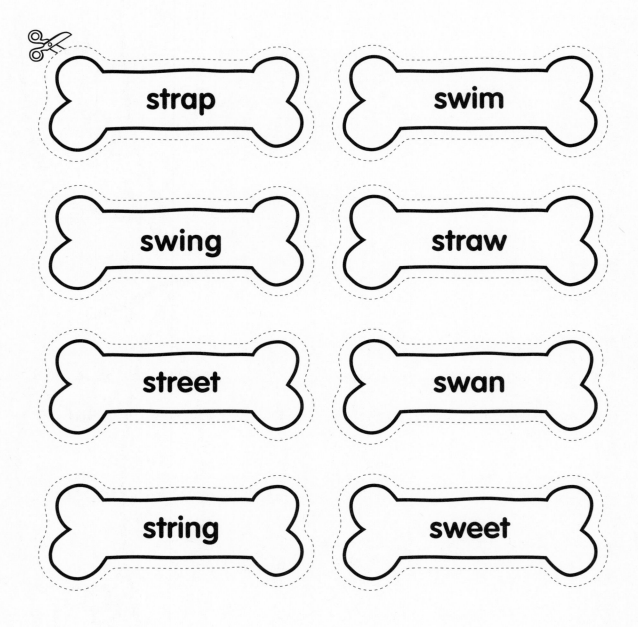

strap

swim

swing

straw

street

swan

string

sweet

Name: _____

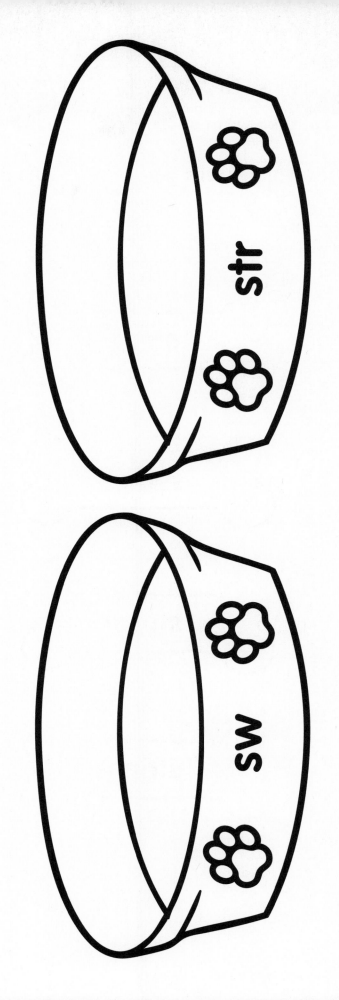

Name: _____

Trace then write each word.

swim

sweet

swan

swing

street

straw

string

strap

PHONICS: Create Your Own

Cut out the cookies. Sort them into the jars.

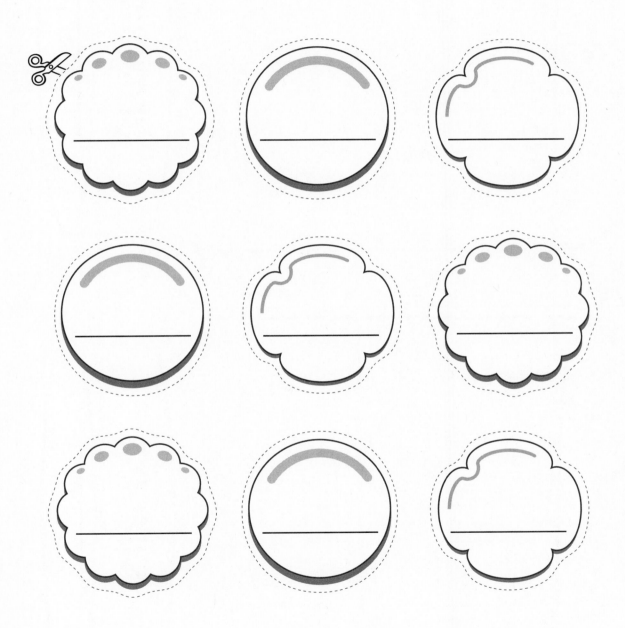

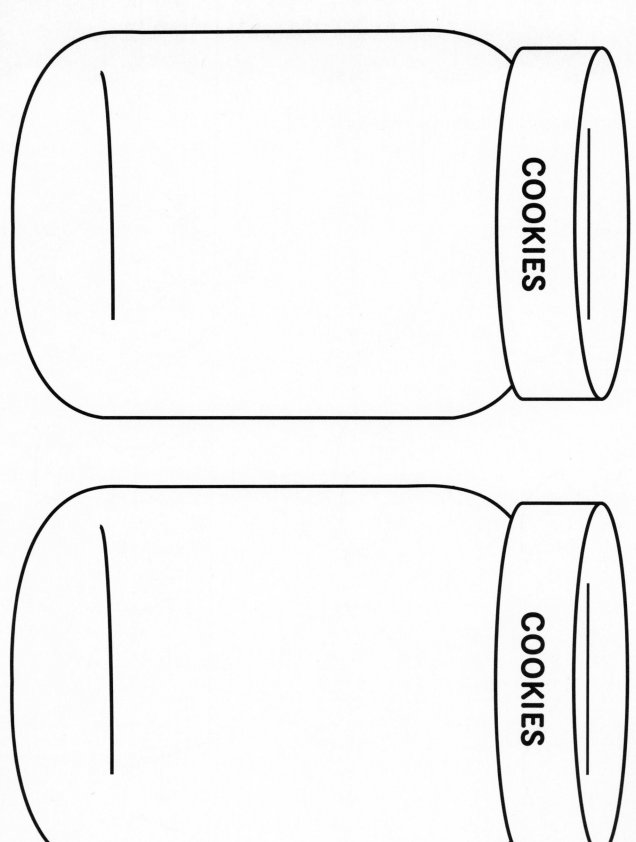

COOKIES

COOKIES

Blank Sorting Templates

Use these templates to customize your activities.

page 10

page 13

page 16

page 19

page 22

page 25

page 28

page 31

page 34

Blank Sorting Templates

page 37

page 40

page 43

page 46

page 49

page 52

page 55

page 58